Xtreme Adventure

POLAR EXPLORATION

BY S.L. HAMILTON

Visit us at
www.abdopublishing.com

Published by ABDO Publishing Company, PO Box 398166, Minneapolis, MN 55439.
Copyright ©2014 by Abdo Consulting Group, Inc. International copyrights reserved in all
countries. No part of this book may be reproduced in any form without written permission
from the publisher. A&D Xtreme™ is a trademark and logo of ABDO Publishing Company.

Printed in the United States of America, North Mankato, Minnesota.
102013
012014

♻ PRINTED ON RECYCLED PAPER

Editor: John Hamilton
Graphic Design: Sue Hamilton
Cover Design: Sue Hamilton
Cover Photo: Corbis
Interior Photos: AP-pgs 6-7, 12, 15, 30-31, 32; Corbis-pgs 22-23 & 29; Getty-pgs 4-5,
8-9, 10-11, 14, 18 (left), 19 (left middle and bottom), 21 & 28; iStock-pg 18 (right top);
NASA-pgs 2-3; National Geographic-pgs 13 & 24-25; NOAA-pgs 20 & 26; Thinkstock-pgs
7 (inset), 9 (inset), 18 (right bottom), 19 (left top, right top & right bottom) , 27, 30
(inset) & 31 (inset); U.S. Coast Guard-pg 1; U.S. Navy-pgs 16-17.

ABDO Booklinks
Web sites about Xtreme Adventure are featured on our Book Links pages. These links are
routinely monitored and updated to provide the most current information available.
Web site: www.abdopublishing.com

Library of Congress Control Number: 2013946160

Cataloging-in-Publication Data

Hamilton, S.L.
 Polar exploration / S.L. Hamilton.
  p. cm. -- (Xtreme adventure)
Includes index.
ISBN 978-1-62403-213-4
1. Polar regions--Juvenile literature. 2. Discovery and exploration--Recreational use--Juvenile
literature. I. Title.
919.8--dc23
                                                    2013946160

CONTENTS

POLAR EXPLORATION

The North and South Poles are two of the harshest environments on Earth. Temperatures never rise above freezing at the South Pole. The North Pole may reach 32 degrees Fahrenheit (0°C) on a "hot" summer day. Still, scientists, explorers, and adventurers are drawn to these icy realms.

XTREME QUOTE – *"We on this journey were already beginning to think of death as a friend."*
— Apsley Cherry-Garrard, Antarctic Explorer 1910-1913

The first humans reached the North and South Poles only a little more than a century ago. Modern transportation and equipment have made it easier for people to reach these frozen wastelands. Yet visitors must carry all the supplies they need to survive. The poles are mostly unexplored. Brave adventurers get to see what few people have seen before.

Tourists from the icebreaker ship Kapitan Khlebnikov *begin an ice hike in Antarctica.*

GETTING TO THE POLES

Early explorers to the poles traveled by ship as far as they could and then crossed the snowy landscapes by walking, skiing, or using dogsleds.

XTREME FACT– Neither the North Pole nor the South Pole are owned by any one nation.

Today, getting to the poles is simpler, but expensive. People travel by ship or plane. Visitors head to the North Pole in the northern hemisphere's summer

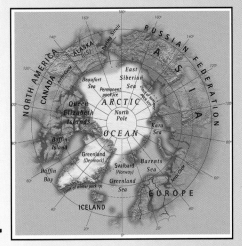

months. Ships called icebreakers cut their way through the Arctic ice. They depart from Alaska, Norway, and Russia. Some adventurers fly to the North Pole. Planes and helicopters land on the ice. People can walk or ski the final distance to precisely 90 degrees north latitude.

An icebreaker ship takes a group of adventurers to the North Pole.

Traveling to the South Pole is more difficult. Cruise ships leave from Australia, New Zealand, Argentina, and Chile, sailing to the frozen continent of Antarctica. Some trips take passengers very far south, but others only take people to the Antarctic Peninsula and Southern Ocean islands. There are also ski plane flights that bring visitors right to the South Pole.

Since the South Pole is really only occupied by scientists, there are not many places to stay. Tent camps are set up during the Antarctic summer, from November to January.

POLAR GEAR

Even during summer, the poles are bitterly cold, usually below freezing. Adventurers must have parkas, snowsuits, mittens, balaclavas, scarves, warm socks, and boots.

Skis and ski poles, water bottles, rope, and backpacks with emergency tents and first aid kits are important for those setting out to explore. A pair of goggles or sunglasses is also important. During each polar region's summer, the sun does not set. The brilliant sunshine can be blinding.

Pole explorers often use pulks to carry their supplies. These small, runnerless sleds glide across deep snow. They are designed to carry a lot of gear in a small space. Items are secured into place using straps. A waterproof cover sits on top.

The lightweight pulk's harness attaches to a person or an animal, such as a dog or reindeer. Pulks are designed to easily maneuver across steep or rough terrain.

XTREME FACT – A larger pulk sled is called an ahkio [ah-kee-oh].

DANGERS

The greatest danger at the poles is the bitter cold. Strong blowing winds can cause "whiteouts," making it impossible to see what's ahead. It is easy to get lost or disoriented even when just a few steps away from camp.

Polar bears are a danger to humans traveling to the North Pole. These powerful bears weigh anywhere from 330-1,200-pounds (150-544-kg). Polar bears have a keen sense of smell. They only live in the Arctic and do not hibernate. They prefer to eat seals, but will attack and eat humans.

XTREME FACT – It's possible to get frostbite and sunburn at the same time at the poles.

North Pole Adventures

Adventurers to the North Pole may see a "pole," but it does not mark the actual North Pole. This is because the Arctic is really just a huge series of ice sheets sitting on top of the ocean. The ice sheets move all the time. A person can set down a pole, but by the next day, it will have moved.

XTREME FACT – The North Pole has one sunrise (at the March equinox) and one sunset (at the September equinox). The sun stays above the horizon in the summer and below the horizon in the winter.

The crew of the United States submarine USS Hampton *posts a sign reading "North Pole" after surfacing in the polar ice cap region. Because Arctic ice sheets move all the time, any marker designating the North Pole never stays in the same place.*

The Arctic polar region is surrounded by land masses. Because of this, many land mammals live in the area. Adventurers may see such animals as muskoxen, reindeer, caribou, foxes, hares, wolves, lemmings, and polar bears. (Polar bears are often considered marine mammals because they live most of their lives on the polar ice pack.)

Muskox

Reindeer

Caribou

Arctic Fox

Wolf

Lemming

Arctic Hare

Polar Bear

The North Pole's surrounding Arctic waters are filled with marine mammals. Whales, porpoises, seals, and walruses may be seen by Arctic visitors. These species capture their prey in the Arctic Ocean. All of these animals are also sometimes eaten by people living in the Arctic region.

Walrus

XTREME FACT – There are NO penguins in the Arctic.

Harp Seal

Narwhal (Whale)

SOUTH POLE ADVENTURES

Adventurers come to Antarctica by ship and by aircraft. After making their way to the southernmost point of the continent, they can touch an actual pole that is called the "ceremonial" South Pole.

XTREME FACT – American scientists working in Antarctica call the continent "The Ice." It is the coldest place on Earth. The South Pole never gets temperatures above freezing.

The cermonial South Pole stands near the Amundsen-Scott South Pole Station. The station is a scientific research base operated by the United States through the National Science Foundation.

Ceremonial South Pole Marker

The "geographic" South Pole is a stationary point on the ground. It is where all the lines of longitude come together at 90 degrees south latitude. This location has to be marked each year. The thick ice sheet that covers the land at the South Pole moves about 30 feet (9 m) each year, taking the marker with it.

GEOGRAPHIC
SOUTH
POLE

ROALD AMUNDSEN

DECEMBER 14, 1911

"So we arrived and were able to plant our flag at the geographical South Pole."

ROBERT F. SCOTT

JANUARY 17, 1912

"The Pole. Yes, but under very different circumstances from those expected."

ELEVATION 9,301 FT.

XTREME FACT – Each year on January 1, surveyors from the U.S. Geological Survey find the geographic South Pole and place a marker. As the ice slides during the year, the marker and the nearby research station are carried along. On New Year's Day another marker is placed at the correct spot atop the ice at the geographic South Pole.

Geographic South Pole Marker

Antarctica is as big as the continental United States and Mexico combined. However, there are no permanent residents. Everyone visits for a period of time.

A marine ecologist poses with killer whales swimming in the Ross Sea, Antarctica.

Very few creatures live near the South Pole. The largest is an insect, a .04 inch (1 mm) midge. Marine mammals such as whales, porpoises, seals, and penguins live near the coastal regions of Antarctica.

Midge

Gentoo Penguins

XTREME FACT – *There are NO polar bears in Antarctica.*

Sea Ice

There are many different kinds of ice formations at the poles. The North Pole sits on thick sheets of ice over the Arctic Ocean. These big ice floes bump into each other, creating piles of tall ridges.

A polar explorer climbs over a pressure ridge made of sea ice on her way to the North Pole.

The South Pole is on the continent of Antarctica. This land mass is surrounded by sea ice. Adventurers arriving by boat view sea ice floating in the surrounding ocean waters. Some ice eventually floats northward and melts.

A ship on its way to Antarctica is surrounded by sea ice.

Glossary

Amundsen-Scott South Pole Station

A scientific research station located at the southernmost place on Earth, the geographic South Pole. It is funded by the United States' National Science Foundation.

Balaclava

Balaclava

A cap-like piece of clothing that clings tightly to the head and neck, leaving only the eyes, and sometimes the mouth, exposed.

Equinox

Two days during the year, usually March 20 and September 22, when the Earth's orbit and the tilt of its axis causes the Sun's rays to shine directly on the equator.

Frostbite

Damage to skin caused by severe cold.

Hibernate

When a warm-blooded animal goes into an extended sleep for the winter. Black bears hibernate, but polar bears do not.

Pregnant female polar bears shelter in dens built into the snow, where they give birth and care for their cubs for about three months.

ICE FLOE
A sheet of ice floating on the surface of the water.

ICEBREAKER
A type of ship built to break surface ice and allow the vessel to pass through the water undamaged.

LATITUDE AND LONGITUDE
A grid system marked in degrees that is used to pinpoint any place on the surface of the Earth. The east-west lines are latitude. The north-south lines are longitude.

NATIONAL SCIENCE FOUNDATION (NSF)
A United States government-run agency that promotes advances in science and engineering. The Amundsen-Scott South Pole Station is funded through the NSF.

SEA ICE
Frozen seawater. Much of the Earth's sea ice is located around the planet's poles.

WHITEOUT
When heavy snow and wind combine to make it impossible for a person to see what is in front of them.

INDEX